Oprah Winfrey

By Wil Mara

Consultant
Nanci R. Vargus, Ed.D.
Assistant Professor of Literacy
University of Indianapolis, Indianapolis, Indiana

Children's Press®
A Division of Scholastic Inc.
New York   Toronto   London   Auckland   Sydney
Mexico City   New Delhi   Hong Kong
Danbury, Connecticut

Designer: Herman Adler Design
Photo Researcher: Caroline Anderson
The photo on the cover shows Oprah Winfrey.

Library of Congress Cataloging-in-Publication Data

Mara, Wil.
  Oprah Winfrey / by Wil Mara.
    p. cm. — (Rookie biographies)
  Includes index.
   ISBN 0-516-21724-0 (lib. bdg.)   0-516-25819-2 (pbk.)
   1. Winfrey, Oprah—Juvenile literature. 2. Television personalities—United
States—Biography—Juvenile literature. 3. Actors—United States—Biography—
Juvenile literature. I. Title. II. Rookie biography.
  PN1992.4.W56M37 2005
  791.4502'8'092—dc22

2004015313

7 8 9 10 R 14 13 12   62

What is your biggest dream?

This is Oprah Winfrey.

Would you like to be on television? Would you like to be a movie star? Would you like to own a company?

Oprah Winfrey has done all of these things.

Winfrey was born in Mississippi in 1954.

She lived on a farm with her grandmother. Her mother and father lived in different places.

When she was 13, Winfrey went to live in Nashville, Tennessee, with her father.

This is Nashville, Tennessee.

This woman is reading the news on the radio, too.

Winfrey worked hard in school. After high school, she went to college in Nashville.

When she was 19, Winfrey got a job on the radio. She read the news.

Later, Winfrey got a job reading the news on television. Barbara Walters read the news on television, too. She was a famous television host.

Winfrey wanted to do the same thing. She was the first African American to have this job.

People liked watching Barbara Walters read the news.

Phil Donahue was a talk show host.

In 1977, Winfrey became a host for a talk show. Winfrey's show was called *People Are Talking*.

There were other talk shows, too. Phil Donahue's show was the most popular.

Later, Winfrey moved to Chicago. She was the host of a new talk show. It was called *A.M. Chicago*.

This is Winfrey on the set of *A.M. Chicago.*

The talk show was a big hit. Soon the show had a new name. It was called *The Oprah Winfrey Show*. This show is still on today.

Have you seen Oprah Winfrey on television?

Winfrey is a good actor, too. She has acted in many movies.

Her first movie part came in 1985. Winfrey was in a movie called *The Color Purple*.

Winfrey played Sofia in *The Color Purple*.

Winfrey works very hard.
She has won many awards
for her work.

What do you get when you spell "Oprah" backwards?

You get "Harpo."

That is what Winfrey calls her company. At Harpo Productions, Winfrey makes her own television shows and movies.

23

O

THE OPRAH

MAGAZINE

SUCCESS!
Define it for yourself

Never Say Never
Amazing women who
prove you can do anything

Fall's delicious
new clothes

What a charming guy!
**OPRAH talks to
TOM HANKS**

OPRAH.COM
SEPTEMBER 2001 $3.50

24

In 1996, Winfrey started a book club on her show. She got many people excited about reading.

Later, she also started her own magazine. It is called *O, The Oprah Magazine*.

Winfrey does many good things for people.

She works to help students go to college. She worked with President Clinton to help keep children safe.

President Clinton   Winfrey

Winfrey and President Clinton are talking.

Winfrey is talking to Laura Bush on Winfrey's show.

Millions of people watch Winfrey's show. They read her magazine, too.

In 1998, Oprah Winfrey was named one of the most important people of the last 100 years.

What do you think?

Words You Know

The Color Purple

Harpo Productions

host

O, The Oprah Magazine

The Oprah Winfrey Show

Index

About the Author

More than fifty published books bear Wil Mara's name. He has written both fiction and nonfiction, for both children and adults. He lives with his family in northern New Jersey.

Photo Credits

Photographs © 2005: AP/Wide World Photos/George Widman: 27; Corbis Images: 11, 12, 31 top left (Bettmann), 3 (LWA-JDC), 7 (Bill Ross); Getty Images: 4 (Carlo Allegri), 20 (Kevin Winter), 24, 28, 31 top right; Retna Ltd/Walter McBride: cover, 23, 30 bottom; The Image Works: 8 (Bob Daemmrich), 19, 30 top (Topham); Time Life Pictures/Getty Images: 15 (Kevin Horan), 16, 31 bottom (Taro Yamasaki).